Object Talks for Preschoolers

by Sandra Crosser

STANDARD
PUBLISHING
Cincinnati, Ohio

The Standard Publishing Company, Cincinnati, Ohio
A division of Standex International Corporation
© 1996 by Sandra Crosser
All rights reserved
Printed in the United States of America

04 03 02 01 99 98 97 96   5 4 3 2 1

Contents

God's Creation

Scripture:

"And God said, 'Let there be light,' and there was light. God saw that the light was good, and he separated the light from the darkness" (Genesis 1:3, 4).

Object: prism

Prisms are available from school supply stores or you may be able to borrow one from a science teacher.
(Teach this lesson on a bright, sunny day.)

(Gather the children near a window and talk about the beautiful sunshine. Ask them to share their plans for this bright, sunny day.)

Light, sunny days are fun because we can be outdoors to play and enjoy the sunshine. We can go to the park or swim at the beach. We can take a walk or go for a bike ride. Could we play outdoors if it were night? Why not? Why would it be hard to play in the dark? We would have to use flashlights or turn on street lights if we wanted to play outdoors at night. That might be a problem.

God made the sun to shine so we would have light. If the sun didn't shine, it would always be night. God made the light for us. When God made the light, He tucked a little secret inside the light. Do you want to see the secret? It is a beautiful secret. God made something beautiful inside the sunlight.

(Hold up the prism.) This is a prism. The prism can help us see the secret God put inside sunlight. I'll hold the prism in the light that is shining through the window. If you look at the floor you will see God's beautiful secret. *(Hold the prism in the sunlight. A rainbow of color will appear on the floor or wall or ceiling depending on how you hold the prism.)*

Do you see God's beautiful secret? What did God tuck inside sunlight? Yes, God put all of the colors inside sunshine. The prism breaks the sunlight into all of the colors God made. God made light so we can see during the day-

5

time. If there were no light, we would not be able to see all of the beautiful colors God made inside the light. Everything would just look black.

God made a beautiful world for us. He gave us sunlight and colors. God has great ideas! God made a world full of beautiful secrets and surprises.

(Leave the prism out so children can try it for themselves at a later time.)

Prayer:
Great God, we thank you for making the sunlight full of beautiful colors. You made a special world for us. Thank you. Amen.

Racial Equality

Scripture:
"God saw all that he had made, and it was very good" (Genesis 1:31).

Object: large sheet of paper, paper dolls, crayons
Before class draw a barely visible outline of a person on a large sheet of paper to use as you talk to the children. You can then darken the parts of the body with a felt marker as you describe them.

(Play a game to get the children into an imagining frame of mind. Have them imagine that they are home in bed all cozy and warm between the covers. Have them imagine eating an ice cream cone. Ask them to imagine it is summer and their skin feels hot so they jump into cold water in a swimming pool and their skin feels nice and cool.)

I'm glad that your imaginations are working today because we are going to take an imaginary, pretend trip. Here we go. Close your eyes and imagine you are going back to a long, long time ago. We're going back a long time before you were a baby, a long time before your dad was born, a long time before your grandma was born. Imagine it is the time before there were any people at all. But remember, God was always there.

Imagine you can see God as He started to make the very first person. *(Draw over your outline of a person on the large sheet of paper. As you draw each body part, say its name.)* He made a head and body. He made arms and legs, hands and feet, fingers and toes. God made all of the inside parts like the heart and stomach and bones. And when God had put His person all together, He covered him with skin. *(Quickly color your drawing of a person using a skin-toned crayon different from the skin color of the children in the group.)*

And God smiled and said, "That's good."

God liked the man He had made. He breathed life into the man so he could move and think and see. God named His man Adam and He said, "That's good."

And then God made a lady person and named her Eve. God thought it would be a good idea for Adam and Eve to become a dad and a mom. So He gave them children. And when the children grew up, God made them moms and dads, too.

God made lots and lots of children who grew up and were moms and dads. God made each baby special. They all looked a little different from each other because God knows all of His children are special. God makes beautiful babies with hearts and bones and eyes and noses. He covers them with skin to hold everything together and protect all of the inside parts. Then God thinks of beautiful colors just like these. *(Hold up a box of crayons.)* God chooses one of these beautiful colors for each baby's skin. And each time He colors a beautiful baby, God says, "That's good!" *(Open a sheet of colored paper dolls.)*

So every time you see all of the beautiful colors of skin that God makes, remember that God loves all colors of people and says, "That's good."

(After the prayer, give each child a strip of four or five paper dolls

to color to remember how many beautiful colors of skin God makes.)

Prayer:
> Dear God, thank you for making each of us special with many beautiful colors of skin. Amen.

When God Says No

Scripture:
> "By this I know that God is for me" (Psalm 56:9).

Object: big sign
> You will need to make a big sign with the word "NO" printed on it. Use large letters.

(Hold up the sign on which you have printed the word "NO.")

Can anyone read this word? It's a very little word but it is very important. *(Wait for responses.)*

How do you feel when your mom or dad says no? Can you tell about a time it happened to you? *(Wait for responses.)* Listen to the story about a boy who said no. See if you can figure out why he said no.

Once there was a boy named Tommy who wanted a puppy more than anything in the world. When he played with Leggos, he thought about how much he wanted a puppy. When Tommy rode his big wheel, he thought about how much fun it would be to have a puppy. When he went to sleep, Tommy even dreamed about playing catch with his puppy. But when Tommy asked his mother if he could have a puppy, she just said, "We'll see."

When Tommy asked his Dad if he could have a puppy, his Dad just said, "We'll see."

Every day Tommy asked his mom or his dad if he could have a puppy, and every day his mom said, "We'll see," and every day his dad said, "We'll see."

Then one day Tommy asked his mom and his dad if he could have a puppy. Instead of saying, "We'll see," Tommy's parents said, "You are ready for a puppy now. You are old enough to take good care of a puppy. You are responsible."

Tommy loved playing with his puppy, Franklin. He fed him and made sure Franklin had water. Tommy trained his puppy to catch a ball and shake hands.

Tommy was always kind to his puppy because he loved him so much. But one day Tommy had to scold his puppy and tell him firmly, "No! No chasing cars!"

Franklin was sad and didn't understand why he was not allowed to chase cars. What do you think Tommy should do? Should Tommy let his puppy chase cars, or should he say, "No?"

Why do you think Tommy wouldn't let Franklin chase cars? Tommy told Franklin, "No! No chasing cars!" Did Tommy still love Franklin?

Tommy said no because he loved Franklin so much and didn't want him to be hurt. Sometimes God says no to our prayers. But God still loves us. Sometimes we don't understand why God says no, but we do know that God always loves us.

Prayer:

Sometimes we don't understand why you say no to our prayers, God. Help us to trust your answer. Thank you for loving us. Amen.

God's Wonderful Creation

Scripture:

"For you are great and do marvelous deeds; you alone are God" (Psalm 86:10).

Object: apple

Bring enough apples for each child to have one. They will enjoy seeing the stars in the apples later at home.

(Ask the children if they like surprises. Let children tell about a time they got a surprise.)

One day I got a wonderful surprise when I was hungry and getting ready to eat something. I didn't eat ice cream or candy or anything like that.

I decided to eat one of my favorite snacks. What do you think it was? *(Wait for responses and then hold up an apple. Demonstrate how you cut the apple in half around the middle.)* As I cut it, I was thinking how good it would taste. Then I saw a big surprise. Right in the middle of the apple was a beautiful star made by the seeds. *(Show the star to the children.)*

I knew that God made apples taste good, but I didn't know He made stars inside them. God surprises me with the beautiful and wonderful way He made all things in the world.

(Ask the children to look for more of God's surprises this week. Suggest that they can tell about what they found or even bring one of God's surprises with them next time. Then follow up with that activity the next time you meet. Give each child an apple as an aid in remembering to look for God's surprises.)

Prayer:

Dear God, it is fun to find your surprises. Thank you for making our world full of wonderful, beautiful surprises. Amen.

God's Commandments Never Change

Scripture:

"Your word, O Lord, is eternal; it stands firm in the heavens" (Psalm 119:89).

Object: game

Bring a familiar child's board game such as Candy Land® to class.

(Ask the children if they have ever played the game. Ask them to tell the names of their favorite games.)

Playing games is great fun. Let's play a game now. *(Invite children to join you in playing a game of Simon Says. Tell the children that before the game begins we need to be certain that everyone knows the rules. Then review the rules with the children. If the leader says "Simon says" then do what the leader tells you. If the leader does not say "Simon says," stand still.)*

Simon says turn around.
Simon says clap your hands three times.
Jump up and down.
Simon says touch your toes.
Touch your shoulders.
Simon says wiggle your fingers.
Pat your head.
Shake your hair.
Simon says touch your knees.
Simon says sit down.

That was a fun game. Now let's play the game a different way. Let's change the rules. This time if you do hear the words "Simon says," stand still. If you don't hear the words "Simon says, " then it's OK to move. Now let's play the game with our new rules. *(Repeat the new rules again.)* Are you ready? Let's go. *(Play the game again using the new rules. End by having the children sit down.)*

It's fun to make up new rules for playing games. We could make up new rules for playing Candy Land® or basketball. We could make up new rules for playing Go Fish. We could make up new rules for playing Duck, Duck, Goose. And we could make up new rules for playing Hide and Seek. It's fun to change the rules in games.

But sometimes people try to change rules that are not part of a game. Sometimes people try to change important rules that Moms and Dads make—rules like, don't play with matches. It's wrong to change those rules. Moms and Dads make rules to keep us safe and well.

God has rules, too. God's rules are even more important than parents' rules. Everyone must follow God's rules. God's rules never change. Do you know one of God's rules? *(Accept any correct responses and reword as necessary. Be sure to include the six listed.)*

1. Love God.
2. Love other people.
3. Obey Mom and Dad.
4. Don't lie.
5. Don't steal.
6. Don't kill.

God's rules are very important. God's rules never change. We can change rules for playing games, but we can never change God's rules. We must always obey God's rules. God's rules are for everyone. When we follow God's rules, we are doing what is right. God's rules help children and grown-ups live right.

Prayer:
Dear God, help us remember your rules every day. Help us follow your rules and live right. Amen.

Praise

Scripture:
"Praise the Lord" (Psalm 150:1).

Object: pom-poms
Before children arrive, cut crepe paper streamers into eight inch strips and tape six streamers together at one end to form a cheerleader type pom-pom. Make a pom-pom for each child.

(Ask the children if they have ever watched a ball game. Talk about what happens at ball games. Tell children you like to watch the cheerleaders. Ask what cheerleaders do.)

We have a team to cheer, too. We're all a team of Christians. We can have cheerleaders, too.

(Invite the children to help you cheer. Start the activity by selecting one child for whom you will cheer. Then give children the pom-poms to shake while they cheer.)

Andrew is a great member of our team. I'm going to cheer for Andrew because he has a great smile. Andrew's smile always brightens my day.

(Then lead the children in the following cheer. Chant it enthusiastically while shaking a pom-pom.)

> Rah, Rah for Andrew.
> Rah, Rah for Andrew.
> Someone on the earth's cheering
> Rah, Rah for Andrew.
> One, two, three, four.
> Who you gonna' cheer for?
> Andrew, that's who!

(Take turns naming positive characteristics and chanting the love cheer for each child. If time is short, cheer for two children at

one time.) When we cheer for someone we are praising them. God wants us to praise Him, too. Let's cheer for God.

(Lead children in naming several of God's characteristics, then chant the above cheer for God.)

Prayer:
Dear God, we praise you for your goodness. We praise you for your strength. We praise you for sending Jesus. You are worthy of our praise. Amen.

A Praise Parade

Scripture:
"Praise him with the sounding of the trumpet, praise him with the harp and lyre, praise him with tambourine and dancing, praise him with the strings and flute, praise him with the clash of cymbals, praise him with resounding cymbals. Let everything that has breath praise the Lord" (Psalm 150:3-6).

Object: rhythm instruments
Before children arrive collect rhythm sticks, triangles, wrist bells, clappers, and any other rhythm instruments you might have. If you do not have access to rhythm instruments, make kazoos by lacing waxed paper over the ends of paper towel or toilet tissue cardboard cores. Secure the waxed paper with rubber bands. Play the kazoos by humming into the open end. Provide enough instruments for each child to have one to play.

Did you ever go to a parade? Were there any bands in the parade? How did the band sound when it was far away? How did the band sound when it was right in front of you? What instruments were playing? How loud were the cymbals? How loud were the horns? How loud were the drums?

I like parades. I like the marching bands and the music. God must like parades, too. Listen to what God says about playing music. *(Read Psalm 150:3-6.)*

God likes it when people play music to praise Him. He likes to hear the horns and cymbals and all of the instruments. Let's play some music for God. We can have a praise parade.

(Quickly show the children how to play the instruments. Then play a familiar, upbeat Sunday school song on a tape or record player. Invite the children to follow you parade fashion around the room playing their instruments to praise God. There is no need to make a formal line. When the background music stops, direct the children to gently place their instruments in a basket on the floor so they can use them again another time.)

Prayer:

Dear God, it is fun making music to praise you. We hope you liked our music and had fun, too. Amen.

Christian Speech

Scripture:

"Pleasant words are a honeycomb, sweet to the soul and healing to the bones" (Proverbs 16:24).

Object: wax lips

You will need a pair of wax lips like the kind sold around Halloween. If you wish, you can give wax lips to the students at the end of class to reinforce the message.

(Have the wax lips in your hand but hidden from sight.)

Get ready to laugh! I found something funny to wear.

When I turn around I'm going to put it on. Are you ready? *(Turn away and put on the wax lips. Then turn around so the children can see you wearing the lips. Tell them where you got the lips and what they're made of. Ask for ideas about how lips are used -- for tasting, kissing, talking, etc.)*

God gave us wonderful lips to do all kinds of good things. But sometimes people use their lips in wrong ways and say mean words. Mean words make people feel hurt and sad. Angry words hurt people, too. God wants us to use our lips to say loving, kind words. Can you think of any loving, kind words? *(Help with suggestions if necessary.)*

(After the prayer, give children wax lips to help them remember that God wants us to use loving, kind words.)

Prayer:

God, help us use our lips to say loving, kind words. Help us use our lips to make people happy. Amen.

God Is Powerful

Scripture:

"Trust in the Lord forever, for the Lord, the Lord, is the Rock eternal" (Isaiah 26:4).

Object: magnet

This magnet trick will be fun for the children to do for parents and friends after class. If possible, provide a small magnet for each child in class.

(Invite the children to watch you do a magic trick. Hold up a large paper clip and a 6" X 6" square of stiff paper.)

I can do a trick. This paper clip is going to be my car and the paper is going to be my road. I can make the paper clip car drive all around the road without falling off, even when the road tips straight up and down. This is really hard, but I think I can do it.

(Out of sight of the children, hold a magnet under the paper. Have the children watch you place the paper clip on top of the paper. Move the magnet to "drive" the paper clip car around the paper road. Then give each child a large paper clip and a 6" x 6" piece of stiff cardboard or old file folder. Invite the children to try the trick. When they are unable to repeat the trick, tell the children the secret.)

I can do the trick because I used a secret power to hold the paper clip and help it move. *(Show the magnet and demonstrate how it works.)*

You couldn't see the magnet because it was behind the paper. But even though you couldn't see the magnet, it had power to pull and move the paper clip. It seemed like magic, but it wasn't. The magnet was just doing what it was supposed to do.

God is like the magnet. God has a lot of power, but we can't see Him. Even though we can't see God, He is very powerful and strong. God's power is working even though we can't see Him.

(After the prayer, give the children small magnets to remind them of God's power.)

Prayer:
Thank you, God, for being so strong. We know you are working even though we can't see you. Amen.

God's Guidance

Scripture:

"Whether you turn to the right or to the left, your ears will hear a voice behind you, saying, 'This is the way; walk in it'" (Isaiah 30:21).

Object: steering wheel

Locate a child's toy that has a steering wheel and dashboard for pretend driving.

(Hold up the toy steering wheel and dashboard.)

Have you ever played with one of these? How do you use it? What do you do with it?

Let's pretend to go for a ride. We only have one toy, but you can pretend that you are driving, too. Are you ready? Let's go. Fasten your seat belts. Put in the key and turn on your engine. Hold on to the steering wheel. Now push on the gas. Here we go. There's a curve in the road, steer to the right. There is another curve in the road, steer to the left. Here comes a stop sign, put on your brakes. No cars are coming, so let's turn right. Slow down for the train tracks. They certainly are bumpy. Let's turn right. Here we go over a bridge and up a mountain. This is a winding road. Turn left. Now turn right. It is starting to rain. Can you turn on your windshield wipers? Turn left at the next road. Now it is getting dark. Can you turn on your lights? Watch out for that dog in the road. Put on your brakes and toot your horn. Whew! That was a close one! We're almost home now. Turn left. Now stop your car. Turn off the windshield wipers and the lights. Turn the key to turn off the engine. We are home and we are safe.

That was fun pretending to drive. If we had been driving real cars, could we have stopped steering to take a nap? Why not? We need to steer the car to keep it on the road. If we stopped steering we would go out of control and crash. The driver needs to stay awake and control the car.

People are a little like cars. We need someone to steer us

so we will stay on the right road—God's road. We need to know when to stop and when to go. We need to know when to turn and go another way. We need someone to stay awake and steer us safely home again.

God is a very good driver. He knows the way we should go to have good lives. God will tell us to stop doing wrong things and do good. He will steer us over bumpy places like when we are sad or angry or hurt. We need to let God steer us in the way we should go and He will bring us safely home to Him.

Prayer:
Dear God, steer our lives so we do the good things you want us to do. Help us stop doing wrong things. Steer us down your road. Keep us safe. We know you are in control. Amen.

Divine Guidance

Scripture:
"Do not fear, for I am with you; do not be dismayed, for I am your God. I will strengthen you and help you; I will uphold you with my righteous right hand" (Isaiah 41:10).

Object: wheels and axle
Collect two wheels and an axle from a child's toy construction set. Show the children one of the wheels.

(Hold up a wheel.)

I found this in a set of toys. Do you know what it is? What are wheels used for? Yes, wheels help things move easier. I'm going to try to roll this wheel to Johnny. Let's see if I can get it to roll straight across the floor to Johnny. *(Roll the wheel. It will most likely roll for a bit, wobble, then fall over and stop rolling.)* What happened when I rolled the wheel? Did it roll to Johnny? It's hard to make the wheel roll where I want it to go. It starts rolling but then it wobbles and falls over. I think I know how to make it roll straighter and not fall over. Let's try an experiment.

(Attach the first wheel to the second wheel using the axle. Then roll it once more.) The wheel didn't wobble and fall over this time? Why not?

Sometimes I feel like this wheel. *(Hold up one wheel.)* I want to roll straight through my days, but sometimes I slow down and wobble and fall over. Some days are just bad days when nothing seems to go right. But when I hook up with God like this *(Attach two wheels with axle once again.)*, God keeps me going His way. God keeps me from wobbling and God keeps me from falling over.

God will hook up with me and help me get through the good days and the terrible days. All I have to do is ask Him. God will hook up with you, too. He'll help you roll through your days. All you have to do is ask Him.

Prayer:
Dear God, please come hook up to our lives and help us roll through our days with you right beside us. Thank you for helping us. Amen.

God With Us

Scripture:
"For I am the Lord, your God, who takes hold of your right hand and says to you, Do not fear; I will help you" (Isaiah 41:13).

Object: picture
You will need a picture of two people holding hands for this object talk.

(Start the lesson with the following movement rhyme. Do the movements with the children as you say the rhyme.)

Wiggle your fingers.
Now wiggle your thumbs.
Wiggle your hands.
Play the drums.
Tap your fingers.
Now tap your thumbs.
Tap your hands.
Play the drums.
Sit on your fingers.
Now sit on your thumbs.
Sit on your hands.
Now play the drums.
Wave your fingers.
Now wave your thumbs.
Wave your hands.
Wave good-bye to the drums.

What else can you do with your hands? *(Show children the picture of two people holding hands.)* Did you ever hold someone's hand? Whose hand did you hold? Why?

When I was a little girl, I thought my dad was the strongest person in the world. He had strong arms and strong, big hands. When my dad took me places that were crowded and busy with lots of people and lots of cars, I would be a little bit afraid. Then my dad would hold my little hand in his big, strong hand. When Dad held my hand, I knew I would be safe.

Now I'm grown up. But sometimes my dad will still take my hand in his big, strong hand. When my dad holds my hand, I know he loves me. Holding hands makes us feel safe and loved. But sometimes when I am all alone and afraid and need to feel safe and loved, my dad isn't there to hold my hand. *(Hold up the Bible.)* In the Bible, almost in the middle, God wrote a special message to you and me. It's a message about holding hands. Listen as I read Isaiah 41:13.

Did you know that God holds your hand in His big, strong hand? You can always feel safe. You can always feel loved. God holds your hand.

Prayer:

Dear God, you know I need to feel safe. You know I need to feel loved. Thank you for holding my hand. Amen.

Personal Nature of God

Scripture:

"I have summoned you by name; you are mine" (Isaiah 43:1).

Object: name tags

Commercial name tags are available, or you can make your own from colored paper and fasten them to the children's clothing with loops of tape.

(Give each child a commercial adhesive paper name tag to peel and wear. If there is time, have children's names preprinted on the tags and pass them out incorrectly. Let the children help you correct the mistake.)

Why do people use name tags? Have you ever worn one before? Why? How do name tags help us?

(Assume a secretive stance and tell the children to listen closely to a very important secret. Use a loud whisper.) God never uses name tags! God already knows your name. He knows Jody and Amanda. He knows Jason's name and all of our names. God knows the names of everyone and He never ever forgets. God knows the name of everybody in the whole world. He knows your mom's name and your dad's name, too. God never ever will forget your name. He must love you very much to always remember your name. Keep your name tag so you can remember that God knows your name.

Thank you, God, for loving me enough to always and forever remember my name. Amen.

Individual Worth

Scripture:
"Yet, O Lord, you are our Father. We are the clay, you are the potter; we are all the work of your hand" (Isaiah 64:8).

Object: buttons
Bring a collection of buttons of various shapes, colors, and sizes to class.

(Show the buttons to the children one at a time. Then give each child a button and tell what it is good for.)

This button is heavy and strong. It is good for buttoning jeans.

This button is very small and plain white. It is just ordinary, but it is a very important button. This simple button is not beautiful, but it does its job well. It holds my shirt together.

This button is very shiny and beautiful. It makes me feel all dressed up. It does a good job of making my dress look beautiful.

This button is very thin and light. It would break easily; it is fragile like glass. But this button is just right for my light, silky blouse. If I were to put a heavier button on my blouse it would tear the cloth.

This big button is for my heavy winter coat. It does a good job of holding my coat together so I'll be warm.

This very tiny button is for a baby's shirt. It has to be very tiny or it wouldn't fit through the little buttonhole. It is small, but it is perfect for the job it has to do.

There are all kinds of buttons. Some are beautiful and

some are not pretty at all. Some are big and strong, but some buttons are very small and fragile like glass. But each button is just right for the job it needs to do.

Buttons are a lot like people. Some people are big and some are small. Some are strong and some are fragile. Some are beautiful to look at and some are just ordinary. But all people are important. All people are important to God even if they are not strong or beautiful. God has a special job for each person. He made each person just right for his/her job. God has a job for you, too. And God made you just right to help Him do His work.

Prayer:
Thank you, God, for making us just right to do your work. You made us different but we are all important. Amen.

God Listens

Scripture:
"Then you will call upon me and come and pray to me, and I will listen to you" (Jeremiah 29:12).

Object: answering machine
An answering machine with a prerecorded message is necessary for this talk. Make it a funny message such as the following: Woof! Woof! This is the doghouse. Spot and I can't come to the phone now. Just bark your message and we'll call you back and howl. Woof!

(Hold up the telephone answering machine with prerecorded message.)

Do any of you have one of these at home? What is it? How does it work? How does it help your family?

I wonder whose answering machine this is. I've got an idea. Let's play the message and find out. *(Play the message on the machine for the children to hear.)*

Do you know that God doesn't have an answering machine? He could have a million if He wanted, but God doesn't need an answering machine. He doesn't even need a telephone. Do you know why? God thinks you are so important that He listens right away whenever you want to talk to Him. He doesn't ever say, "Wait a minute." He doesn't ever say, "Call back later." He doesn't ever say, "I'm too busy now." God thinks you're so important that He listens right away every time you talk to Him. God is great! God loves you a lot.

(After the prayer, give children stickers that say, "God loves me." Stickers of this kind are available in most Christian bookstores.)

Prayer:
God, thank you for loving us so much that you always listen when we talk to you. Amen.

God's Greatest Commandments

Scripture:
"Jesus replied, 'Love the Lord your God with all your heart and with all your soul and with all your mind. This is the first and greatest commandment. And the second is like it: Love your neighbor as yourself'" (Matthew 22:37-39).

Object: big chart
Before class, prepare the chart with the rules listed below.

(Hold up the chart with rules on it. Cover up the rules but let the title, "Rules," show. Then tell this story.)

Rules:
1. Use soap.
2. Pick up dirty clothes.
3. Flush.

When I was a little boy/girl, we had rules at our house. This word says rules. *(Point.)* Do you have any rules at your house? Tell me the most important rule. *(Now uncover the rest of the rules chart.)*

These were my family's rules for the bathroom. Help me read them. *(Point as you read each rule.)* These rules were important at our house, especially to my mother. When my brother/sister and I followed the rules for the bathroom, my mother was happy and we didn't get into trouble. That made everyone happy. Things just worked out better for everyone.

God has rules, too. Jesus said God has two big, most important rules of all. If everyone follows God's most important rules, then everyone will be happier. Things will work out better for everyone.

Does anyone know God's biggest, most important rules?

(After taking responses, tell the children that God's biggest rule is, "Love God." The next most important rule is, "Love One Another." Ask the children to suggest how we can show that we love one another. If there are few responses, offer a suggestion such as: play fair, help people who are hurt or sad, help do work at home, be friendly, share, etc.)

(After the prayer, give each child a button or sticker that says, "Love one another." Such buttons and stickers are available at most Christian book and gift shops.)

Prayer:
God, help us to love one another. Help us be kind and helpful to everybody. Help us follow your rules. Amen.

Christian Strength

Scripture:
    "But love your enemies, do good to them" (Luke 6:35).

Object: barbell
    If a real barbell is not available, you can use a toy one
    or substitute another piece of exercise equipment and
    adapt the talk to fit it.

*(Hold up a small barbell or other small piece of exercise equip-
ment.)*

Look at what I found in the garage. I'm so excited about
finding this barbell! I'm going to get really big, strong muscles now that I have a barbell. I know I'll get very strong
because I saw a man on TV lifting barbells and he had
huge muscles.

Get ready now. I'm going to lift it. Don't be surprised if
my muscles get so big that my shirt buttons pop right off.
Here I go. I'm lifting it now. Watch!

*(Lift the barbell one time, inspect your muscles, and then act dis-
appointed.)*

Something is wrong. My muscles didn't grow big. I'll try
one more time.

(Try once again and then act disappointed.)

This barbell must be no good! Or did I do something
wrong? Can you tell me why my muscles didn't grow
when I lifted the barbell?

*(If the children do not think about the importance of practice, ask
them if they think your muscles will grow if you lift the barbell
every day for a long time.)*

Muscles need to be used hundreds of times to make

them grow strong. I'll need to practice with the barbells many times every day for a long time if I want my muscles to grow. It will be hard work. God wants us to have strong bodies, but he also wants us to be strong Christians, too. Sometimes it's hard work to be a strong Christian. We have to practice to grow into strong Christians. Strong Christians are kind and loving and helpful to everyone. What can you do to practice being a strong Christian? We need to practice being kind and loving with our friends. But here's the hard part—we need to practice being kind and loving with mean people, too. We need to practice being kind and loving to brothers and sisters and friends and even people who are mean to us. Then we will grow into strong Christians like God wants us to be. Practice over and over by sharing and helping and taking turns.

Prayer:
God, help us to grow into strong Christians. Help us to always be kind and loving with everyone, even when it's hard. Amen.

Personal God

Scripture:
"People were also bringing babies to Jesus to have him touch them. When the disciples saw this, they rebuked them. But Jesus called the children to him and said, 'Let the little children come to me, and do not hinder them, for the kingdom of God belongs to such as these'" (Luke 18:15, 16).

Object: VIP badge
Provide a badge on which you have written in large print VIP. You can make one out of paper or cardboard covered with aluminum foil.

(Hold up the VIP badge.)

(Be dramatic with introduction of the badge.) This is a VIP badge. Only someone who is a VIP can wear this badge! Do you know what a VIP is? A VIP is a Very Important Person. *(Point to the letters as you say the words.)* Do you know anyone who is a VIP?

(Take the children's suggestions. If they cannot think of a VIP, ask them if Michael Jordan, the President, Mr. Rogers, the pastor, or the school principal could be a VIP.)

Yes, these are all very important people. God thinks they are all VIPs. God knows all of the VIPs. God knows billions of VIPs. Billions of people live on this earth and God says every one of them is a VIP. Famous people are very important to God. But in God's eyes, everyone is famous. God knows every person on earth and God thinks every one of us is a VIP. Little babies are very important to God. Little children are very important to God. Big kids are very important to God. Moms and dads and grandmas and grandpas are very important to God. You are very important to God. You are one of God's VIPs. This is how I know children are VIPs.

One day there were some grown-up VIPs talking to Jesus about important business. When some children came around to see Jesus, the men said, "Get those children out of here. We have important business to talk about. Make those children go away." But Jesus didn't like it when the men chased away the children. Jesus said, "Let the children come to me," and He called all of the children to come to Him. Then Jesus told the men that they must not stop the children from coming to Him. Jesus knows that all children are VIPs.

(Give each child a badge because they are all VIPs to God.)

Prayer:
Dear God, we are glad to know that you think each person is very important. You care about each one of us. You care about children. Thank you. Amen.

Born Again

Scripture:

"In reply Jesus declared, 'I tell you the truth, no one can see the kingdom of God unless he is born again'" (John 3:3).

Object: play dough

Gather enough blue and yellow play dough for each child in your class to have a small ball of each color.

(Show the children a ball of blue play dough. Ask them if they have ever played with play dough. Ask what they made.)

I like my ball of blue play dough. Blue is a very nice color, but it is only one color. Everything I make with this blue dough is all the same color, just blue. It isn't very much blue dough and it can only make blue things. Sometimes I wish I had more colors of play dough. Then I could make more beautiful things.

(Look around and act surprised.) Oh, look! Here's another can of dough to play with. I wonder if it is blue, too. Let's open it and find out. *(Open can.)* It's yellow. This is great! Now I can make blue things and yellow things. Watch.

(Knead together the blue and yellow play dough. When the play dough turns green, act surprised and pleased.)

Look at what happened to the blue play dough. It turned a beautiful green. The yellow dough changed the blue dough to green. What a beautiful change!

When people don't know Jesus, they are like the ball of blue play dough. But when people ask Jesus to come into their lives, something wonderful happens. Just like the yellow play dough changed the blue to green, Jesus changes our hearts and we are more beautiful, more kind, more loving. He makes us different. When we ask Jesus to come live in our hearts, He becomes part of us and makes us more like Him. We become kinder and more loving. Jesus wants to come into our hearts and change us into better people.

(Give each child a small ball of blue play dough and a small ball of yellow play dough to knead together. Emphasize that the blue ball is like a person and the yellow ball is like Jesus.)

When Jesus comes into our hearts, we change to be more like Him.

(If it would be a problem for children to play with the dough after the lesson, send the dough home in individual plastic sandwich bags.)

Prayer:
Jesus, come live in my heart and change me. Make me more like you. Amen.

God Forgives

Scripture:
"For God so loved the world that he gave his one and only Son, that whoever believes in him shall not perish but have eternal life" (John 3:16).

Object: eraser
As a follow-up, you may wish to give each child a small eraser to take home.

(Hold up a letter you have written in pencil.)

I have a problem and need your help. I have been writing a letter to my friend but I made a mistake and ruined the letter. I am sorry and sad that I ruined the letter. I told *(Insert a name.)* about it and she gave me one of these. *(Hold up a large eraser.)* The problem is, *(Name.)* left and didn't tell me what this thing is or what to do with it. *(Ask children if*

31

they can tell you what it is and what you should do with it. And after their suggestions, quickly use the eraser to correct the mistake in your letter.)

Thank you for helping me. I am much happier now that I have erased the mistake and made my letter right again.

Did you know that God has a great big eraser? When we do something wrong, like hitting or being mean, we make a mistake. We feel sorry and God wants to help us feel better. We can ask God to use His big eraser to forgive us and get rid of the mistake. We can ask Him to erase the wrong things we do so we will feel better and God will feel better, too. But we have to remember to ask God to use His eraser when we need Him to forgive the wrong things we do.

(Give each child an eraser to keep as a reminder to ask God to use His big eraser for them.)

Prayer:

Thank you, God, for erasing the wrong things we do when we are sorry. Amen.

God's Gift of Jesus

Scripture:

"For God so loved the world that he gave his one and only Son, that whoever believes in him shall not perish but have eternal life" (John 3:16).

Object: Christmas gifts

Cut out as many paper hearts as there are children in the group. Attach a sticker picturing the baby Jesus to each heart. Place the decorated hearts in a gift wrapped box.

(Hold up the gift wrapped box.)

Christmas is a special time for giving and receiving gifts.

Are there any gifts at your house? Have you been making any gifts to give people? It is exciting to plan what to give.

When we give someone a gift, it shows we love them. A long time ago God gave the very first Christmas gift ever. God planned the most special gift. He chose the perfect gift to last forever. Then one night long ago, God gave his special gift to all the people of the world. The angels knew about the gift and they were so excited that they gathered in the sky and sang songs about God's special gift. Do you know what God's gift was? *(Wait for responses.)*

God's gift showed how much He loves us. God gave us the baby Jesus on that very first Christmas. Jesus was God's gift.

When you open gifts this Christmas, remember that God gave the first Christmas gift ever. It was a gift of love. God gave us the baby Jesus.

There is something inside this box to help us remember God's gift. *(Open the gift and take out the heart pictures. Give a heart picture to each child.)* Take this picture of Jesus home. Look at it and remember God's first and best Christmas gift. Let's thank God for the gift of Jesus.

Prayer:
Thank you, God, for your Christmas gift. Thank you for Jesus. Thank you for loving us. Amen.

Human Worth

Scripture:
"For God so loved the world that he gave his one and only Son, that whoever believes in him should not perish but have eternal life" (John 3:16).

Object: stuffed animals
Acquire two stuffed animals. Choose one that is obviously old and ragged and another that looks new. Introduce the stuffed animals by name to the children.

Invite children to tell about a favorite stuffed animal of their own.

(Hold up the new-looking stuffed animal.) This animal is soft and fluffy. He has bright eyes and smells good. He has pretty fur and a new ribbon around his neck.

(Hold up the tattered stuffed animal.) This animal is a little dirty and his fur is worn. He is missing one of his eyes and he doesn't smell very good. If you could choose to have one of these stuffed animals for your own, which one would you choose? Why? *(Accept several responses.)*

These stuffed animals are a lot like people. Some people look terrific with combed hair and nice clothes. They smell good and are nice to look at. But some people are not so nice to look at. Some people are old and don't look so good anymore. Some people have strange hair and old clothes. Some people have worn-out bodies and even parts that don't work. Some people don't smell very good.

(Hold up the tattered animal.) Some people are like this old stuffed animal. They don't look as pretty as this one. *(Hold up the new-looking stuffed animal.)* But someone has loved this old animal for a long time. Someone hugged him tightly at night and took him outdoors to play. Someone loves this animal very much even though he isn't pretty and new any more. Someone loves this animal so much that they don't even care that his eye is missing and his fur is dirty.

That's how God loves His people. God doesn't care how we look. He loves all of us. God loves good-looking people and God loves people who are not so good-looking. God loves people who have to use wheelchairs because they can't walk. God loves people who can't see or hear very well. God loves people who are fat and God loves people who are skinny. He loves people with beautiful hair and He loves people with no hair. God loves rich people and God loves poor people. God chooses all people for His own. He loves us all the same. God chooses everyone!

We need to be like God. We need to love all people.

Prayer:
God, help us to be like you. Help us to love everyone.
Amen.

Salvation

Scripture:
"'No,' said Peter, 'you shall never wash my feet.' Jesus
answered, 'Unless I wash you, you have no part with
me'" (John 13:8).

Object: shoes
Bring an old pair of athletic shoes and a pair of sandals
to class.

(Hold up an old pair of athletic shoes.)

These are my favorite shoes. They have taken me lots of
places. They took me walking on the beach and got sand
inside. They took me to the woods and got mud inside.
They took me running and got sweaty and smelly inside.
They took me splashing through puddles and got water
inside. Where have your shoes taken you? *(Accept several
responses.)*

A long time ago when Jesus walked on earth, there were
no shoes like ours to take Him where He wanted to go.
Jesus had to wear this kind of shoes. *(Hold up a pair of sandals.)* Jesus and His friends had to wear sandals everywhere they went. Because there were no cars or trucks or
airplanes or buses or bicycles to ride, Jesus and His
friends had to walk everywhere they wanted to go. It
must have been hard to walk in sandals all of the time.
Jesus and His friends walked everywhere: they walked in
the sandy desert; they walked in the rocky mountains;
they walked in the stones by the water; they walked in the
mud and the puddles. How do you think their feet looked
after all that walking in sandals? How do you think their

feet smelled after all that walking?

One night Jesus did something that surprised His friends. He got a pan of clean water and a towel and washed His friends' dirty, smelly feet. Jesus washed the dirt and the dust and the mud off of His friends' feet. And then He wiped them dry.

But Jesus' friend, Peter, didn't want Jesus to wash his feet. Peter knew that Jesus was God's Son. Peter didn't want Jesus to have to hold his dirty feet and smell the sweat on his skin. Peter thought Jesus was too special and too important to bend down and wash his dirty, smelly feet. But Jesus said He must. Jesus must wash everyone clean.

When we do things that are wrong, it is like we walk in mud and get all dirty. When God looks at us, He sees we are dirty. Jesus is the only one who can wash away the wrong things and make us clean again. When we do wrong things, we need to ask Jesus to wash away the wrong things just like He washed away the dirt on His friends' feet. Jesus wants to wash away all of the wrong things we do. Let's ask Him.

Prayer:
Dear Jesus, only you can wash away the wrong things we do. Please come wash away all of the wrong things we have done. Make us clean for God. Amen.

Living in Love

Scripture:

"A new command I give you: Love one another. As I have loved you, so you must love one another" (John 13: 34).

Object: dried or sandpaper starfish

If possible, secure a dried starfish for this talk. If one is not available, you can make a starfish out of sandpaper or papier-mâché.

(Place the dried starfish in a small box and pass it around. Invite the children to touch it gently. Ask them to describe how the starfish's body feels.)

When a starfish is alive, its body is soft and not stiff. When it is alive, it moves in the water by waving its arms like this. *(Wave your arms up and down gently and rhythmically. Then invite the children to move their arms like a starfish, too.)*

A starfish needs to be in water in order to be soft enough to move and live. When a wave pushes a starfish out of the water and onto the land, it can't live. The sun dries out the starfish's body and it becomes hard and stiff. If we try to move the starfish's arms, they will break off because they are not in the water. God planned for starfish to live in water.

God has a plan for people, too. God planned for people to live in love. When we live in love, we are good and kind to other people. We share and take turns. When we live in love, we are happy. God planned for starfish to live in water, and God planned for people to live in love. When a starfish gets out of the water, it gets all dried up. When people get out of love, they get mean and unhappy. We need to be good and kind to other people so we can all live in love.

(Give children photocopies of your real starfish to help them

37

remember to live in love. Or cut starfish shapes out of sandpaper to help them remember that we get rough and stiff when we live out of love just like the starfish gets rough and stiff when it gets out of water.)

Prayer:

Dear God, sometimes we forget your plan for us. Help us remember to be good and kind by sharing and taking turns. Help us live in love like you planned. Amen.

When Bad Things Happen

Scripture:

"Now we see but a poor reflection as in a mirror; then we shall see face to face. Now I know in part; then I shall know fully, even as I am fully known" (1 Corinthians 13:12).

Object: large hand mirror

If you wish, bring a small pocket mirror (plastic, not glass) for each child in class.

(Smudge a large hand mirror with dirt so that it does not reflect a clear image. Hold the mirror in front of your face and pretend to have difficulty combing your hair. Move the mirror to several different angles and squint into it.)

I am so upset! I am so frustrated! I am so exasperated! I cannot seem to comb my hair. Something is wrong with this mirror. Look! *(Show the dirty mirror to the children and have them tell you what is wrong.)*

Have you ever felt upset and frustrated and exasperated? Why?

Sometimes I feel upset, frustrated, and exasperated

when bad things happen. I don't understand why bad things happen.

I felt upset, frustrated, and exasperated when I was sick and had to stay in bed. I don't understand why people get sick.

I felt upset, frustrated, and exasperated when my gold-fish died. I don't understand why animals die.

I felt upset, frustrated, and exasperated when my shirt got torn and my bicycle broke. I don't understand why my favorite things get ruined.

There are lots of things that make me upset, frustrated, and exasperated because I don't understand why they happen. But when I get to Heaven, I will understand why bad things happen. Jesus said it is like this dirty mirror. Now we try to understand but we can't. It's like looking in a dirty mirror. We can't see clearly. We can't understand.

But when we get to Heaven, we will understand every-thing. Jesus will tell us the answers, and then it will be like looking into a clean, shiny, new mirror. We will understand why bad things happen. We will understand everything.

(Give each child a small pocket mirror to take home. The mirrors will help them remember that when we get to Heaven, Jesus will help us understand everything. He will sit with us and answer all of our questions.)

Prayer:

Jesus, we know you will answer all of our questions when we get to Heaven. It will be like looking in a clean mirror. Help us feel better when bad things make us upset, frustrated, and exasperated. Thank you. Amen.

Strength Through God

Scripture:

"I can do everything through him who gives me strength" (Philippians 4:13).

Object: eggs

Prepare a hard-boiled egg by soaking it overnight in vinegar. The shell will soften, allowing the egg to bounce rather than crack if the egg is dropped.

(Hold up the egg.)

Boys and girls, say hello to my friend, Humpty Dumpty. Humpty Dumpty is a good egg, but he does have one problem. Do you know what his problem is? There is a rhyme that tells us about Humpty Dumpty's problem. Say the rhyme with me.

Humpty Dumpty sat on a wall.
Humpty Dumpty had a great fall.
All the king's horses and all the king's men
Couldn't put Humpty together again.

Why couldn't they put Humpty Dumpty together again? What happens when an egg falls? Did you ever see an egg fall? What a mess! Why does it make such a mess when an egg breaks? What do you think would happen if I dropped this egg onto the floor right now? How many people think it would break? Let's try it and find out. *(Drop the egg from a height of one or two feet.)*

What happened? Were you surprised? This is an extra strong egg. Most eggs would break if we dropped them onto the floor. Eggs are fragile. They break easily. But our extra strong egg didn't even crack. It just hit the floor and bounced. I'll tell you the secret for making an extra strong egg. Can you keep a secret? *(Whisper.)* The secret is, put a hard-boiled egg in a bowl of vinegar and leave it there all night. The vinegar makes the egg shell soft so it will bounce. Maybe your mom or dad will let you try it at home.

People are a lot like eggs. People are fragile, too. Sometimes we think that problems in life are too hard for us. Sometimes we feel like we are ready to crack like an egg. When we are upset or frightened or hurt or angry or sad, we can feel like we are going to break. It would be nice if we could put people in vinegar and make them stronger, but that only works with eggs.

There is a way to make people stronger. There is a way to make people bounce back when trouble comes. Eggs get stronger when we put them in vinegar. People get stronger when we put them in God's love. Vinegar made the egg stronger. God's love makes people stronger.

Prayer:

Dear God, make us strong so we can bounce back when trouble comes. You are our strength. Amen.

Pray

Scripture:

"Pray continually" (1 Thessalonians 5:17).

Object: pretzels

Small individual bags of pretzels will help the children remember to say their prayers.

(Hold up a brown paper bag in which you have concealed a package of twist-type pretzels. Give the children three or four guesses to figure out what could be hidden in the bag. Give clues such as the following: there are lots of them; they are salty; they are brown and have curved shapes; they are my favorite snack. Show the children the bag of pretzels and invite them to name their own favorite snack.)

I really like the way pretzels taste, and I'm thankful for all of the good food God gives us to eat. Let me tell you a story about the first person who ever made a pretzel.

A long, long time ago there was a man who loved God very much. This man was called a monk because he spent his whole life working for God. The monk lived in a big house with a lot of other monks, so he called them his brothers. All of the brothers helped do the work in the big house. Some of the brothers cooked, some cleaned the house, and some planted flowers and gardens.

One day the cooking monk mixed together some flour and yeast and sugar and water to make some dough. He rolled the dough into long, skinny ropes like he always did. But then he had an idea.

The cooking monk took one of those long, skinny ropes of dough and bent it carefully into a special shape. Then he made more shapes. When he finished, he sprinkled the special shapes with tasty salt and baked them in the oven until they were golden brown.

When the other monks saw the beautiful pretzels, they were very surprised. The pretzels looked just like the monks' arms when they were folded during prayers. *(Hold up a pretzel and show the children how to fold their arms in prayer like the monks did.)* Now whenever I see a pretzel, I am reminded to say my prayers.

(Give children small bags of pretzels to help them remember to say their prayers.)

Prayer:
Dear God, sometimes we forget to pray. Help us remember to pray to you every day. Amen.

God's Blessing
of Love

Scripture:
"All Scripture is God-breathed and is useful for teaching, rebuking, correcting and training in righteousness" (2 Timothy 3:16).

Object: paper hearts
Cut out paper hearts and print the words, "God Bless You," on them. With loops of tape, fasten many of these colored paper hearts to your clothing or to a big apron.

(Stand in front of the children with a big smile on your face.)

I am excited because Valentine's Day will soon be here. I have been cutting out hearts to give to everyone. What are you doing to celebrate Valentine's Day? *(Take one paper heart off of your clothing.)*

When I give this valentine, I'm going to say, "Happy Valentine's Day. God bless you."

I love to say, "God bless you," because it is very, very special. The words on this heart say, "God Bless You." If you want to give very special valentines, be sure to say, "God bless you." It is a special prayer of love.

God gave each of us a valentine that says, "God bless you." Here it is. *(Hold up a Bible.)* God wrote His Bible for you and you and you. The Bible is our most special valentine because God made it for us with His love.

(One at a time, remove the hearts from your clothing. Give them to the children individually as you say, "God bless you.")

Prayer:
Dear God, thank you for giving us the Bible so we can be blessed and learn about your love. Bless you. Amen.

Faith in God's Presence

Scripture:

"Now faith is being sure of what we hope for and certain of what we do not see" (Hebrews 11:1).

Object: balloon

Provide a large balloon for the talk and a small balloon for each child in class.

(Hold up a deflated balloon and tell the children that you are upset.)

I went to the store and asked to buy a balloon, but when I got home and opened the package there wasn't a big, pretty, bouncy balloon in it like the one I saw in the store. All I got was this flat balloon. *(If the children do not volunteer the idea that you should blow up the balloon, ask them if they can tell you what to do. Then blow up the balloon and ask them to tell you why the balloon changed. Let a little air squeak out of the balloon and act surprised at the noise.)*

I did not see the air come out of the balloon. Did you? Let's try again and watch for the air to come out. *(Let a little more air squeak out of the balloon.)* Did you see the air come out? I didn't either. *(Ask the children what they think will happen if you let go of the balloon so all of the air can come out. Then, try it.)*

We did not see the air come out of the balloon, but we know it did come out because the balloon is flat again. We cannot see air, but we can see what air does when we put it in a balloon and let it out. God is like the air. We cannot see air and we cannot see God either, but we can see what air does. We can see what God does, too. We can see the beautiful things that God makes. We can see His animals and His rainbow and stars. We can see all of the people God made. What else can we see that God made?

(Give children balloons to remind them that God is like the air. We cannot see Him, but we can see what He does.)

Dear God, we can't see you now, but we know you are here. We see all of the things you have done. Amen.

Faith and Works

Scripture:
"In the same way, faith by itself, if it is not accompanied by action, is dead" (James 2:17).

Object: straws

Obtain a plastic cup and lid from a fast food restaurant. Be sure the lid has a slit for a straw. Before children arrive, place soft serve ice cream in the cup and close it tightly with the lid. Insert a drinking straw through the lid.

(Hold up the restaurant cup.)

There is something very good inside this cup. It is cold and thick. Can you guess what it is? *(Accept several guesses.)* Yes, there is ice cream in this cup. It is very thick, just the way I like it. I'd sure like some of this ice cream, but the lid is stuck and I don't have a spoon. I guess I can't have any ice cream today. *(Look disappointed.)*

I wish the lid weren't stuck and I wish I had a spoon. Can you help me think of what to do? *(Children will most likely suggest that you use the straw.)*

Use the straw? Why didn't I think of that? I'll just blow into this straw. *(Do it.)* That straw must be broken. I blew into it and nothing happened. I didn't get any ice cream at all. I'm so disappointed!

(If children do not volunteer that you should suck through the straw, ask them what you could try next.)

OK, I'll try sucking through the straw. *(Do it.)* This is

hard work. I need to suck really hard to get the ice cream into the straw. It's hard work, but I think I can do it. Yummy! I finally got some. It tastes great! Thanks for telling me what to do. I had to work hard but it was worth the try. Sometimes we have to work hard to get a good thing. We have to try. That's one way God works in our lives. Sometimes God wants us to work hard and try. We can't just ask God to give us all of the good things in our lives. God expects us to work hard and try for good things.

We have to work hard to have friends. We have to work hard to get along with brothers and sisters. We have to work hard to have happy families. We have to work hard to be Christians. Sometimes we have to work hard for good things.

(After the prayer, give each child a cup of soft ice cream with a lid and straw if you wish.) Enjoy the treat and remember that sometimes we need to do a little work to get something good.

Prayer:
> Dear God, we will try to remember that we need to work hard for good things. We will try to work hard at being friends and getting along with brothers and sisters. Amen.

God's Presence in Time of Sorrow

Scripture:
> "Come near to God and he will come near to you" (James 4:8).

Object: butterfly
> Locate a dead butterfly. Place it in a box on a bed of cotton and cover completely with clear plastic wrap.

(Hold up box so children can see the dead butterfly.)

I love to watch butterflies, and I am really sad because I found this beautiful dead butterfly.

It's dead and can't fly around any more. It's wings don't move. It can't eat or sit on flowers any more.

Have you ever felt sad? Why?

I don't like feeling sad. I'd rather have good feelings, like feelings of being happy or excited or surprised or proud. Sometimes people don't understand if I'm feeling sad. But God always understands my feelings because God feels happy sometimes and God feels sad sometimes, too. God always understands and knows how we feel. God will come extra close to us when we feel sad.

Prayer:

God, you must love us very much to understand our sad feelings and happy feelings. Thank you for coming extra close to us when we are feeling sad. We love you, too. Amen.

God Is Love

Scripture:

"God is love. Whoever lives in love lives in God, and God in him" (1 John 4:16).

Object: measuring devices

Collect a variety of measuring devices such as a plastic measuring cup, measuring spoons, a ruler, a bathroom scale, calipers, clock, etc. Also, bring enough small rulers for each child to have one, or you can make photocopies of a ruler if you wish.

(Show the measuring devices you have chosen to bring to class. Ask the children to tell how each item is used.)

Which one of these things would you use to measure how much sugar to put into cookie dough? Which would you use to measure how much you weigh? Which would you use to measure how long your foot is? Which would you use to measure how much you love your mom?

Tell me how much you love your mom. I love my mom so much I can't even measure how much.

Jesus said that God's love is even bigger than we can say. God loves us even more than we love our families. God is love.

(After the prayer, give each child a ruler or a photocopy of a ruler to remember God's love is so big that we can't even measure it.)

Prayer:

Dear God, we're glad that you are always loving us. Your love is too big to measure. We love you, too. Amen.